I0605990

For Baby Ligibel, Henry, Rosie, and Evelyn—
your future is big.

Grateful acknowledgment to Rachel R. Renne, a doctoral candidate studying big sagebrush ecosystems at the Yale School of the Environment, for sharing feedback on the text and illustrations.

Millbrook Press™
An imprint of Lerner Publishing Group, Inc.
241 First Avenue North
Minneapolis, MN 55401 USA

For reading levels and more information, look up this title at www.lernerbooks.com.

Designed by Athena Currier.
Main body text set in ITC Avant Garde Gothic Std. Typeface provided by Adobe Systems.
The illustrations in this book were created using pastel, colored pencil, collage paper, and a Wacom pen tablet.

Library of Congress Cataloging-in-Publication Data

Names: Fagan, Kirbi author illustrator
Title: The big empty : a sagebrush survival story / Kirbi Fagan.
Description: Minneapolis : Millbrook Press, [2025] | Audience term: juvenile | Audience: Ages 5–10 Millbrook Press | Audience: Grades 2–3 Millbrook Press | Summary: "Spare poetic text and gorgeous illustrations introduce readers to big sagebrush, a vital plant in the American west. It feeds and shelters many animals, and after a wildfire, it grows again and thrives once more" —Provided by publisher.
Identifiers: LCCN 2024054185 (print) | LCCN 2024054186 (ebook) | ISBN 9798765627242 library binding | ISBN 9798765682494 epub
Subjects: LCSH: Big sagebrush—Ecology—West (U.S.)—Juvenile literature | LCGFT: Poetry
Classification: LCC SB615.S2 F34 2025 (print) | LCC SB615.S2 (ebook) | DDC 583/.983—dc23/eng/20250214

LC record available at https://lccn.loc.gov/2024054185
LC ebook record available at https://lccn.loc.gov/2024054186

Manufactured in Guang Dong, China by Dream Colour Printing
1-1012025-52106-2/20/2025

THE BIG EMPTY

A Sagebrush Survival Story

KIRBI FAGAN

Millbrook Press / Minneapolis

People passing by call this land the big empty.

But I call it home.

Beyond the haze they leave in their tracks,
a secret world springs to life.

In this nowhere land,
my evergreen leaves, tender with water,
are a thirsty mother's only hope.

I am nourishment
when there is nothing else.

Birds peck at my fallen seeds
while I cradle turquoise jewels in my arms.

I am a nursery
under the wide western sky.

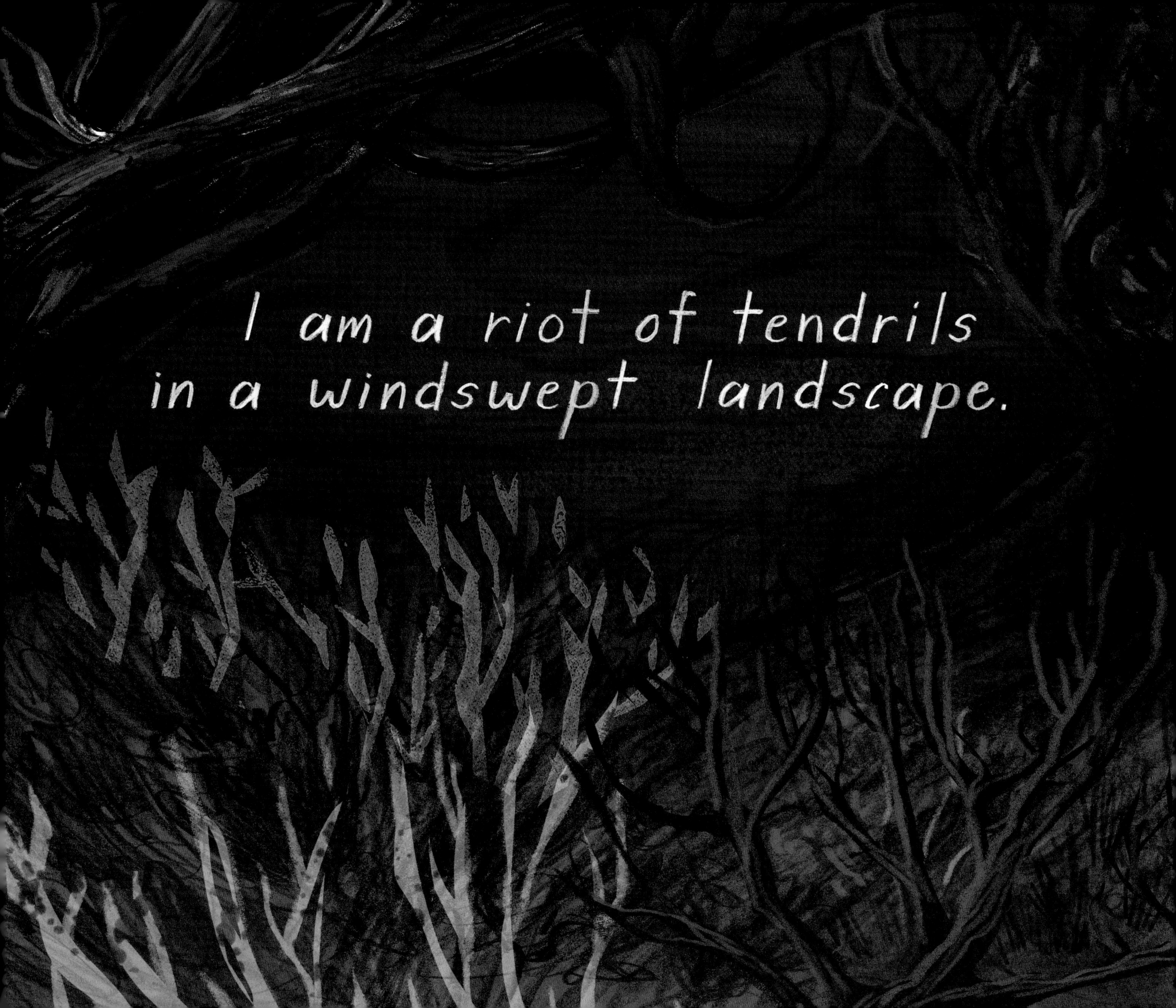
I am a riot of tendrils
in a windswept landscape.

Critters burrow beneath my trunk
and scamper under every twist.
Even my fallen branches are homes.

My gnarled limbs cast wild shadows,
cloaking hunters searching for prey.

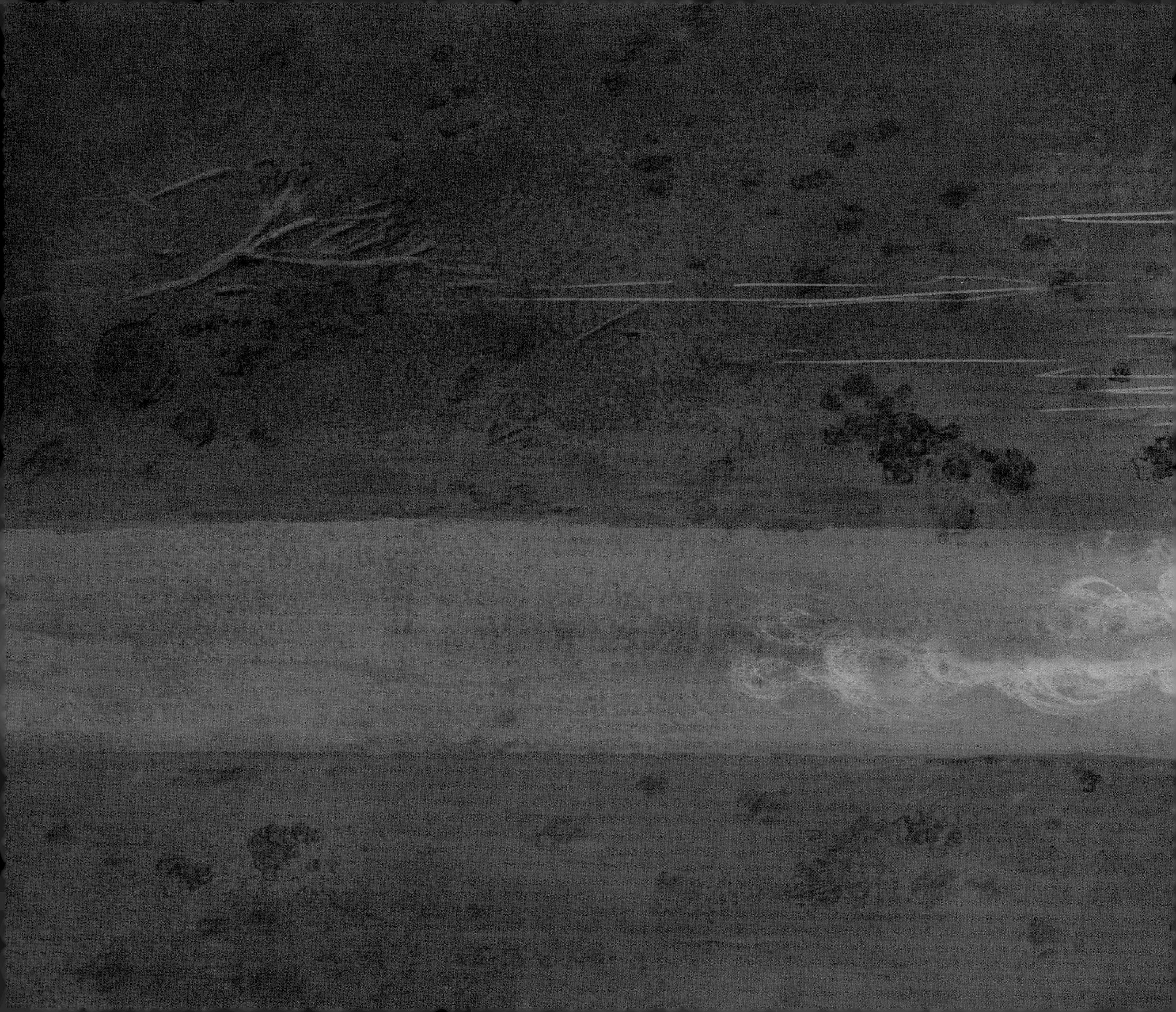

Here, no one is safe.
A flicker in the faraway sky is a threat to everyone.

Even me.

As fire rages, my leaves burn and animals scatter.

Afterward, my home looks as lonely as the moon.

Yet beyond the ash, my seeds are everywhere.

I am hope.

When I'm strong enough,
I will bloom bursts of yellow.
I will thrive again.

I am called big sagebrush.
I am the one that grows where nothing else will.

In a land of sun and fire,

I am life.

MORE ABOUT BIG SAGEBRUSH

North America's western shrublands may appear barren and empty, but in reality, they are a diverse and complex habitat. The sagebrush ecosystem covers many millions of acres, and it supports about 350 wildlife species.

Big sagebrush is a hardy plant that grows in rugged areas with little rain or snow. It provides shelter and food for a variety of animals. It's known as a nurse plant because it offers shade and protection to other young plants growing nearby.

Big sagebrush plants have a number of adaptations that help them thrive. They produce certain chemicals to make their leaves undesirable to insects. Their leaves are covered in tiny hairs that protect them from drying out in the heat and wind. Big sagebrush plants grow small flowers in late summer and early fall, which produce large amounts of pollen that is spread by the wind. Some animals also eat the flowers and seeds.

Big sagebrush has a specialized configuration of roots. Shallow roots spread wide to gather spring and summer rain. Other roots grow deep underground to bring up water that other plant species growing nearby can't reach.

Fire poses serious risks. Big sagebrush is slow to recover after wildfire, relying on wind to blow in seeds from other areas. Invasive grasses tend to grow more quickly than sagebrush, and those grasses, in turn, increase the risk for future fires. While the threats to sagebrush are ongoing, sagebrush's resilient nature gives reason to be hopeful for the future of the plant and the hundreds of species that rely on it.

Scientists have identified more than twenty different types of sagebrush, with big sagebrush being the most widespread. The main kinds of big sagebrush are Wyoming sagebrush, mountain sagebrush, and basin sagebrush. Each subtype grows best in different terrain and conditions. Ongoing research has shown that plants are still thriving at sixty to eighty years of age, and the oldest known big sagebrush are more than two hundred years old!

ANIMALS OF THE BIG EMPTY

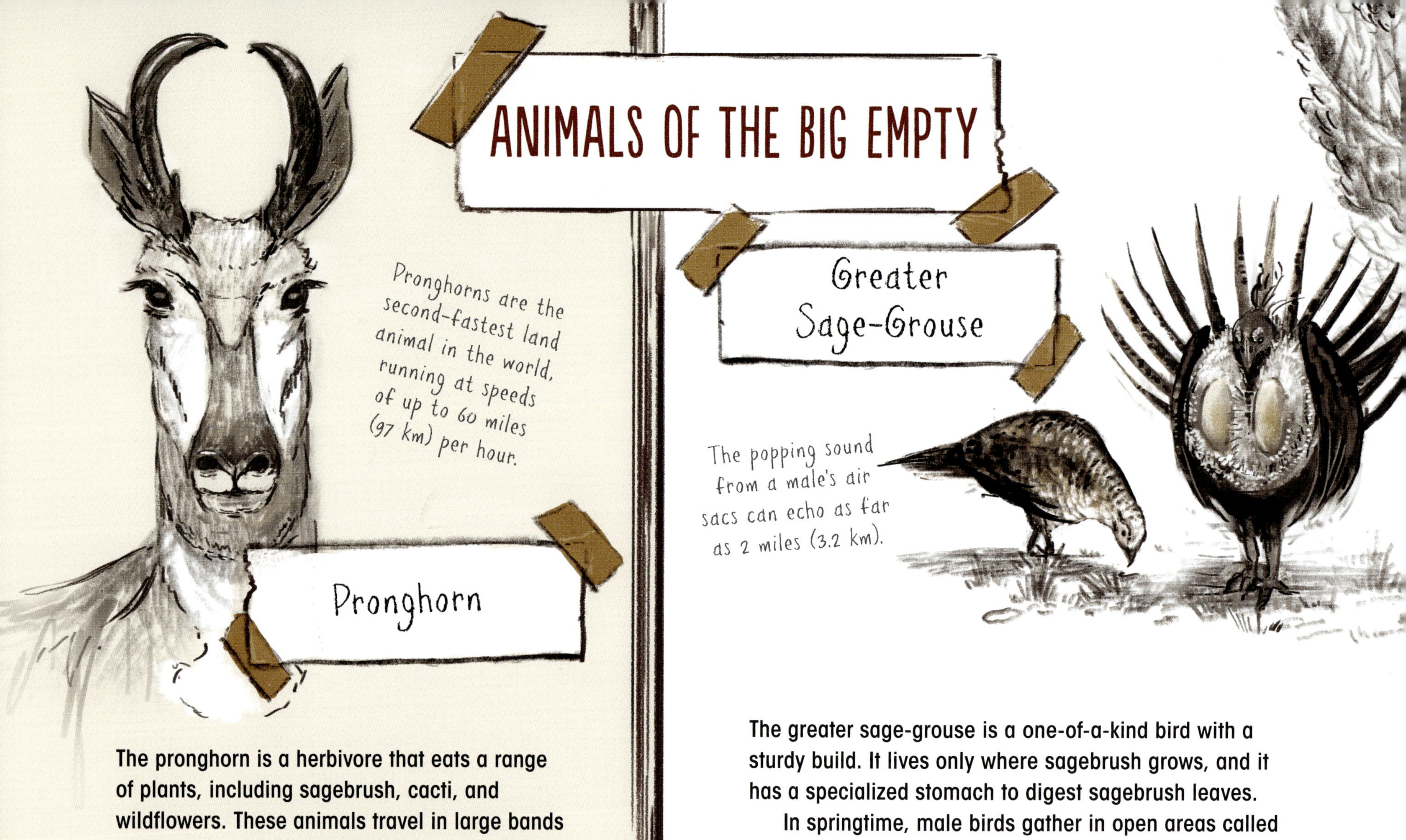

The pronghorn is a herbivore that eats a range of plants, including sagebrush, cacti, and wildflowers. These animals travel in large bands in the winter and in smaller bands in the summer.

Mother pronghorns give birth in late spring, and twins are common. The fawns stay hidden in tall grasses for the first several weeks of their life, spending much of their time without their mothers. After those early weeks, mothers and fawns join the herd.

The greater sage-grouse is a one-of-a-kind bird with a sturdy build. It lives only where sagebrush grows, and it has a specialized stomach to digest sagebrush leaves.

In springtime, male birds gather in open areas called leks to attract females. The males fan out their pointy tail feathers and puff out their chests. They rapidly inflate and deflate air sacs on their neck, creating distinctive popping sounds. Females watch the displays and then choose a mate. After mating, the females lay their eggs under the protective branches of the sagebrush.

Pygmy Rabbit

The pygmy rabbit lives in areas of dense sagebrush, relying on it for both food and shelter. The twists and turns of the sagebrush act like a mini forest for these rabbits, which weigh less than 1 pound (0.5 kg).

Pregnant female pygmy rabbits dig secret underground burrows in the loose soil. Mothers give birth in their burrows and will cover the entrances with brush and soil for additional protection. The tiny young are especially vulnerable to predators.

Bobcats, foxes, coyotes, birds of prey, and others all hunt pygmy rabbits.

Sage Thrasher

The sage thrasher spends summers in sagebrush. Similar in size to a robin, it can be hard to spot in the dense foliage. It eats insects, including ants and grasshoppers, and berries.

Thrashers build their nests on or near the ground, often in the branches of big sagebrush plants. Mothers lay four to five eggs, which are a brilliant turquoise color with brown speckles. Both parents build the nest and feed and care for their young.

Thrashers will defend their territory by flying low to the ground in zigzags while singing.